Contents

Introduction

What this book contains	3
How to set, mark and interpret the tests	3
Helping your child sit tests	4
What to do with the results	4

English

Testing your child's English	6
Spelling picture	12
Spelling text	13
Comprehension test – fiction	14
Comprehension test – non-fiction	20
Reading test	24
Writing test	25
Answers	26

Mathematics

Testing your child's mathematics	33
Test (Levels 2/3)	36
Practice pages	52
Number and algebra Level 2	52
Number and algebra Level 3	54
Shape, space and measure Level 2	56
Shape, space and measure Level 3	58
Handling data Level 2	60
Handling data Level 3	61
Answers	62

Text © ST(P), Sean McArdle and Wendy Wren 1997

The right of ST(P), Sean McArdle and Wendy Wren to be identified as the authors of this work has been asserted by them in accordance with the Copyright, Designs and Patents Act 1988.

The authors and publishers wish to thank the following for permission to use copyright material: Puffin Books for the excerpts from *Dragon Ride* by Helen Cresswell, Penguin Books 1987; *1996 Key Stage 1 English Tasks: Reading and Writing Teacher's Handbook*, SCAA, 1995, Ref. KS1/95/322.

All rights reserved. No part of this publication may be reproduced or transmitted in any form or by any means, electronic or mechanical, including photocopy, recording or any information storage and retrieval system,without permission in writing from the publisher or under licence from the Copyright Licensing Agency Limited. Further details of such licences (for reprographic reproduction) may be obtained from the Copyright Licensing Agency Limited of 90 Tottenham Court Road, London W1P 9HE.

Designed by Ian Foulis & Associates, Saltash, Cornwall
Illustrated by Katerina Sardella and Mike Miller

First published in 1997 by
Stanley Thornes (Publishers) Ltd
Ellenborough House
Wellington Street
CHELTENHAM GL50 1YW

97 98 99 00 / 10 9 8 7 6 5 4 3 2

A catalogue record for this book is available from the British Library.

ISBN 0-7487-3069-9

Printed and bound in Great Britain by The Baskerville Press, Salisbury, Wiltshire

Introduction

What this book contains

During your child's last year in infant school (Year 2) he or she will sit Key Stage 1 National Assessment Tests in the two core subjects: English and mathematics. These tests take place in school over a period of about a week during May and the results are reported back to you and are also passed on to the teacher of the Key Stage 2 class your child will attend. For each of the subjects your child will be given a mark in the form of a level. Most children will perform in the range of Levels 1–3 by the end of Key Stage 1 with an average performance being roughly Level 2.

The tests are a valuable measure of your child's performance in school. Not only will they be influential in the school's assessment of your child's progress, they may also be your child's first experience of sitting formal written tests. It is extremely helpful if that first experience can be a positive one.

This book provides you with one complete set of practice papers for each of the subjects with the principle aim of preparing your child confidently for the tests. Each set of papers will:

- provide test questions similar to those in the National Tests for Levels 1–2a in English and 1–3 in maths in the National Curriculum.

- give your child practice in sitting the tests: working to a set time, getting familiar with the format and style of the tests and developing effective test strategies.

- give you a broad guide to your child's likely level of performance within Levels 1–3 of each subject.

- give you an idea of strengths and weaknesses in your child's learning.

How to set, mark and interpret the tests

Each set of papers allows you to set, mark and level your child's work in the subjects without any prior knowledge of the National Curriculum. First read the detailed advice on setting the papers; then set the test. When your child has finished each paper use the answers to mark it. Then use the conversion box at the end of the answers to get an idea of National Curriculum level.

INTRODUCTION

Helping your child sit tests

As well as practising the content of the tests, one of the key aims of this book is to give your child practice in working under test conditions. All the tests are timed and your child should try to complete each one within the given time. In order to make best use of the tests, and to ensure that the experience is a positive one for your child, it is helpful to follow a few basic principles:

- Talk with your child first before embarking on the tests. Present the activity positively and reassuringly. Encourage your child to view doing the papers as an enjoyable activity which will help, always making him or her feel secure about the process.

- Ensure that your child is relaxed and rested before doing a test. It may be better to do a paper at the weekend or during the holidays rather than straight after a day at school.

- Ensure a quiet place, free from noise or disturbance, for doing the tests.

- Ensure that there is a watch or clock available.

- Ensure that your child understands exactly what to do for each paper and give some basic test strategies for tackling the task. For example:

  - Try to tackle all the questions but don't worry if you can't do some. Put a pencil mark by any you can't do, leave them and come back at the end.

  - Make sure you read the questions carefully.

  - Go straight on to the next page when each is finished.

  - Try to pace yourself over the allowed time. Look over the whole paper first to get an idea of how many questions there are. Don't spend too long over one question.

  - Use all your time.

  - If you have any time over at the end go back over your answers. This is particularly important if you are doing one big piece of work, such as writing a story.

- Taking the time to talk over a test beforehand and to discuss any difficulties afterwards will really help your child to gain confidence in the business of sitting tests.

- However your child does, ensure that you give plenty of praise for effort.

What to do with the results

The tests in this book and the results gained from them are only a guide to your child's likely level of performance. They are not an absolute guarantee of how your child will actually perform in the National Tests themselves. However, these papers will at least allow your child to get practice in sitting tests; they will also give *you* an insight into the strengths and weaknesses in their learning.

If there are particular areas of performance which seem weaker, it may be worth providing more practice of the skills required. It is also valuable to discuss any such weaknesses with your child's class teacher, and to seek confirmation of any

INTRODUCTION

problem areas and advice on how to proceed. It is always better to work in partnership with the school if you can. Above all ensure that you discuss these issues with your child in a positive and supportive way so that you have their co-operation in working together to improve learning.

ENGLISH

Testing your child's English

Introduction

Key Stage 1 tests are an important part of monitoring and assessing the progress and levels of attainment of 7-year-olds and, as such, should be seen as a diagnostic tool. Any kind of 'testing' can be intimidating, so letting children practise what they are expected to do serves two purposes.

1. It gives you more than just a 'snap shot' of your child's performance at one particular time.
2. It helps children become familiar with what is required, thus making them less likely to underachieve through nervousness in a new situation.

This book has one complete test divided into the following sections:

- Spelling test – pictures and text

- Comprehension test – fiction and non fiction

- Reading test – fiction

- Writing test

It is important to note that in the actual Reading test, your child will be given a choice of books. It is impossible to recreate this, but to ensure that the reading passage is within a familiar context, it follows on from the Comprehension test which your child should do first.

The different sections of the test can be given individually to allow children to practise the areas in which they are weakest, or as a whole.

The introductory notes for each section summarise the design of the test and the instructions you should give to your child. You can reword the instructions as you think fit. These notes are followed by the different sections of the test and answers, marking and assessment criteria.

Setting the spelling test

1 This test is suitable for children whom you think are working within Level 2 or above in writing.

2 The tests are designed to enable children to show their ability when they are asked to concentrate solely on spelling.

3 The tests contain a range of words commonly known by 7-year-olds and have been taken mainly from the Group 1 list of *Essentials in Teaching and Testing Spelling* by Fred J Schonell, 1985.

4 Give your child a copy of the test and a pencil. Tell him/her to rub out or cross out answers they wish to change.

Picture spelling tests

1 Discuss the large picture with your child and the small pictures around it.

2 Make sure your child knows what each picture represents.

3 Ask your child to write the name of each small picture in the box underneath. You can remind him/her what the pictures are if he/she has forgotten.

Text spelling tests

1 The text test is thematically linked to the picture test so the children should feel comfortable with the context.

2 Ask your child to listen to you as you read out the complete text, which you will find on p. 26. You may find it helpful to make a copy of the passage to read out.

3 Ask your child to look at the text and note that some of the words are missing. These words are in bold type in the passage on p. 26.

4 Explain that when you read the text again your child should write in the missing words as you go along.

5 Reread the text, pausing to let the child write in wherever a word has been missed out. Each missing word may be repeated three times.

Setting the comprehension test

1 Each test is designed so that it can be completed in one session, but you may decide to have a break between the fiction and non-fiction passages.

2 There is no time limit for the test.

3 Give your child a copy of the test and a pencil. Tell him/her to rub out or cross out answers they wish to change.

4 Do not help your child with the reading of the text. However, you may help with the spelling of the answers they wish to give. Do not penalise your child for spelling errors but encourage him/her to be as careful as possible.

5 Tell your child to read a page at a time and to try to answer the questions at the bottom of the page. Remind them that they:

- can rub out/cross out answers they wish to change,
- should tick only one box for each question,
- will find the answers on the same page as the question,
- should try every question.

6 Throughout the test you can remind your child of what he/she should be doing, i.e. read a page then answer the questions at the bottom of the page; turn over and read the next page, etc.

Setting the reading test

The test is designed to enable children to demonstrate their ability to:
- read aloud from a text;
- show what they have understood;
- give a personal response.

In the actual Key Stage 1 test, the child reads from a whole book. As it is impossible to recreate this exactly, the reading test here is a continuation of the comprehension passage, and as such should follow the comprehension test.

The reading test begins where the comprehension test finished. Each test has a marking grid and suggested questions.

1 Explain to your child that what he/she is going to read is part of the story *Dragon Ride* which he/she has already done some work on.

2 Reread the beginning of the story from the comprehension test. It is very important that the early part of the story, before the reading passage begins, is shared with your child, so that he/she can become familiar with the structure of the story and any names or specialised language used.

3 Ask your child to read aloud the passage and attempt any unfamiliar words.

4 Use the grid on page 28 to mark the following:
- **O** for any words omitted;
- **T** for any words you have to tell your child (words which the child needs in order to retain the sense of the passage);
- the exact word your child says when he/she makes an incorrect attempt.

5 Record the strategies your child uses to attempt to read unfamiliar words, whether they are **T** (told) or not, using the following codes:

Ph = phonic	knowledge of print symbols and sound patterns
G = graphic	knowledge of parts of words or consistent letter patterns, e.g. help for helping
S = syntactic	a grammatically sensible substitution, e.g. his/her, me/he
C = contextual	a sensible substitution within the meaning of the text as a whole, e.g. dirty for dusty
Sc = self correct	evidence of successful use of reading strategies

Discussing the book after reading

Following your child's reading you should discuss the whole text, i.e. the comprehension and reading passages, with your child.

Level 1

The discussion should focus on your child's ability to understand the text and identify aspects which he/she enjoyed or found interesting.

Questions which you might ask or adapt can be found following the marking grid for the passage, on page 29.

What to look for
A range of appropriate responses to some of these questions will provide evidence of your child's understanding and response to aspects of his/her reading.

Level 2

If your child is responding well, move on to explore his/her understanding of, and ability to express opinions about, the main events or ideas in the text. Begin by asking your child to tell you what has happened in the story so far and to talk about what might happen in the rest of the story.

Use the retelling to initiate a discussion during which your child is given the opportunity to respond to the story so far. Ask a range of questions with the aim of encouraging your child to talk about the meaning and significance of what he/she has read in order to gather evidence of his/her understanding of and response to the story.

Some examples of the sorts of question you might ask can be found following the marking grid, on page 29.

What to look for
Responses to a range of questions of the type suggested will provide evidence of your child's understanding of and response to the story.

You should observe, for example, whether your child:
- has understood the main events or ideas in the book;
- is able to express opinions or feelings about main characters;
- is able to comment on reasons why the story was enjoyable.

Setting the writing test

In school the writing test will be undertaken by all children who are being assessed at the end of Key Stage 1. It may be developed from the stories the children have encountered in the comprehension and reading tests or from other work in the classroom. In this book, the writing test is developed from the work done on the comprehension and reading tests.

The writing test provides a broad assessment of your child's independent writing, covering his/her ability to communicate meaning to a reader, together with a developing awareness of punctuation and the conventions of spelling and handwriting.

What to do

1 The grid on page 25 gives suggestions as to the types of writing the children could do based on the comprehension and reading passages. From the grid, choose one idea as a focus for the writing, which may be a story or a piece of non-narrative writing.

2 Introduce the writing test to your child by:

- encouraging him/her to plan his/her writing;

- considering who the writing is for and the appropriate ways of organising it, e.g. letter, instructions, story;

- discussing themes, characters, ideas;

- exploring appropriate words and phrases;

- rereading the story;

- researching additional information.

3 This support must stop short of telling your child what to write.

4 You can give your child a general reminder about punctuation.

Spelling picture

Spelling text

_____ cat was in the _____ this morning. It was

_____ by a tree looking _____ .

It could _____ a bird's nest and it wanted to _____

the tree to _____ the bird.

The _____ bird left the nest and flew to the _____ of

the tree.

I got the cat and put it in the _____ .

Comprehension test – *Fiction*
Dragon Ride

All Jilly wanted in the world was a dragon. Luckily, it was

her birthday next month. She would be seven.

She told her brother, Ben. She didn't really think he could afford

a dragon (he was only five), but she asked him anyway.

---

1 What did Jilly want for her birthday?

☐ a brother ☐ a dragon

☐ a dog ☐ a bike

2 How old was Ben?

_____

'What – one that puffs fire?' he asked her.

'Yes,' replied Jilly. 'One that puffs *lots* of fire. Not at everybody, mind you. Just at the people I want it to puff at.'

She already had a long list of people who would get scorched if she got her dragon.

---

3 What did Jilly want the dragon to do? ✔ ✏

☐ fly   ☐ sing

☐ puff fire   ☐ dance

4 Did Jilly want the dragon to puff at everybody?

'How do you know it wouldn't puff at me?' Ben asked.

'I'm not getting you a dragon. I'm getting you —'

'Shush!' Jilly shrieked. 'Shush! Don't tell!'

Ben clapped his hand to his mouth.

If you had a secret, Ben was the last person in the world that you told it to. He had just nearly given away his own secret!

---

5 Ben put his hand on his ✔ ✎

☐ mouth ☐ head

☐ knee ☐ arm

6 What did Ben nearly give away?

_____

Jilly had always secretly thought how marvellous it would be to have a dragon as a pet. She loved the look of them. She loved their shiny green scales and curly tails. And on most pictures she had ever seen of dragons, they seemed to be smiling. Even when they were puffing out great clouds of smoke and fire, there always seemed to be that faint, secret smile.

---

7 What did Jilly like about dragons? ✔︎ ✎

_____

_____

8 What did dragons always seem to be doing?

☐ crying   ☐ eating

☐ running   ☐ smiling

Dragons, she knew, didn't grow on trees. In fact, up till now, she had thought it was impossible to get a dragon at all. Then she saw something about them in her comic. It told you about people who keep them as pets. It told you what to feed them on, and how often to take them for walks. Jilly cut out the page and kept it carefully at the back of her stamp album.

---

9 Jilly found out about dragons ✔ ✎

☐ in a book ☐ in a newspaper

☐ in a comic ☐ on TV

10 Where did Jilly keep the page about dragons?

_____

This was one of Jilly's birthday cards.

Happy Birthday

Hope you like the game. Couldn't find a dragon.

Lots of love,
Ben

---

11. Who sent the birthday card?

12. How old was Jilly?

13. What did Ben buy her?

14. What couldn't Ben find?

Comprehension test – *Non-Fiction*
Dragons

Introduction

People have told stories about dragons for a very long time.
In stories, dragons were very often large and green, and fire came out of their noses. They were not very friendly and people were afraid of them.

1 Dragon stories have been told for ✔️ ✏️

☐ a long time   ☐ a short time

2 What did dragons look like?

_____

_____

Where did dragons come from?

We do not really know why people began to tell stories about dragons.

People who sailed to far away lands saw strange animals. When they came back they tried to draw them and say what they looked like. They made these animals bigger and more frightening than they really were.

Maybe this is how stories of dragons started.

---

3 People who sailed to different lands saw

☐ dragons

☐ strange animals

4 What did people say about the animals they saw?

_____

_____

_____

St George and the dragon

There is a famous story about a man called George who had to fight a dragon to save a princess.

The people in the town had given all the sheep to the dragon for food, but he would not go away.

The dragon wanted to eat the people from the town. Just as the dragon was about to eat the King's daughter, George rode up on his white horse and killed it.

5 What did the people feed the dragon at first? ✔ ✎

☐ cows ☐ goats

☐ sheep ☐ pigs

6 Who killed the dragon? ✔ ✎

☐ the King ☐ George

The Komodo dragon

There is a lizard living today which is called the Komodo dragon. It is the biggest of all lizards and can grow to 3 metres long and weigh 135 kg.

It has a very strong neck and body and a powerful tail. It has short, strong legs and attacks and eats smaller lizards.

It gets its name from the island on which it lives which is Komodo Island.

7 How long does the Komodo dragon grow? ✔ ✎

☐ 6 metres   ☐ 3 metres

☐ 135 metres ☐ 10 metres

8 What does the Komodo dragon look like? ✎

_____

_____

_____

Reading test
Dragon Ride

Jilly asked for the dragon when the family was sitting round having dinner.

'It's all I want in the world!' she said.

'That'd be handy,' said Mr Tonks. 'No need to buy another box of matches ever again!'

'Now come along, Arthur,' said Mrs Tonks. 'Don't tease the child.'

'Fry the bacon on its breath,' went on Mr Tonks. 'Just think of that!'

'I'm not joking, Dad,' said Jilly. 'I really, really want a dragon. I don't want any other presents. In fact, if I can have a dragon, I don't even mind not getting any presents next Christmas, either.'

Writing questions grid

Idea	Example	Dragon Ride
Extending and adapting ideas or language patterns	A further episode of the story Characters used in a different setting Using a repeated phrase	An adventure Jilly has with the dragon
Informative writing	A data base entry or leaflet	A poster advertising dragons for sale
Personal response/review	Comments to tell other children about the book or to recommend it	Writing to a direct question: Write about why you liked *Dragon Ride*
A personal account	Inspired by characters or events in the book	Write about a pet you would like
Alternative versions	Own versions of the story/ alternative viewpoint	Tell the story from Ben's viewpoint
Letter writing	Questions or a letter to the author, illustrator or a particular character	Letter to Jilly asking how she would look after a dragon
Instructions	Explaining how to do or make something	Rules for feeding a dragon
Expressing opinions	Giving own viewpoint about behaviour or events	Is Jilly sensible or silly for wanting a dragon?

ENGLISH ANSWERS

Spelling picture

Spelling text

My cat was in the **garden** this morning. It was **sitting** by a tree looking **up**.

It could **see** a bird's nest and it wanted to **climb** the tree to **catch** the bird.

The **mother** bird left the nest and flew to the **top** of the tree.

I got the cat and put it in the **house**.

Conversion of score into National Curriculum levels

Marks	0 – 4	5 – 10	11 – 14	15 – 18
NC Level	1	2C	2B	2A

Comprehension test

Notes

1. Tick boxes: one mark is gained for each correct answer ticked. If your child has ticked more than one box, no mark should be given.
2. Single word/short response: You will need to make decisions about the answers given by your child. Try to take account of what your child actually means, even though it may not be well expressed. If your child's response does not answer the question, it should be marked as incorrect even though you may understand why your child wrote it.
3. Do not penalise your child for poor handwriting.

Dragon Ride

1	a dragon	1 mark
2	five	1 mark
3	puff fire	1 mark
4	no	1 mark
5	mouth	1 mark
6	his own secret	1 mark
7	shiny green scales **or** curly tails **or** smiling	1 mark
8	smiling	1 mark
9	in a comic	1 mark
10	at the back of her stamp album	1 mark
11	Ben	1 mark
12	seven	1 mark
13	a game	1 mark
14	a dragon	1 mark

Dragons

1	a long time	1 mark
2	large **or** green **or** fire came out of their noses	1 mark
3	strange animals	1 mark
4	bigger than they were **or** more frightening	1 mark
5	sheep	1 mark
6	George	1 mark
7	3 metres	1 mark
8	strong neck **or** strong body **or** powerful tail **or** short, strong legs	1 mark

Conversion of score into National Cuurriculum levels

Marks	0 – 6	7 – 12	12 – 17	18 – 22
NC Level	Level 1 not achieved	Level 2C achieved	Level 2B achieved	Level 2A achieved

Reading test

Jilly asked for the dragon when the family was sitting round having dinner.

'It's all I want in the world!' she said.

'That'd be handy,' said Mr Tonks. 'No need to buy another box of matches ever again!'

'Now come along, Arthur,' said Mrs Tonks. 'Don't tease the child.'

'Fry the bacon on its breath,' went on Mr Tonks. 'Just think of that!'

'I'm not joking, Dad,' said Jilly. 'I really, really want a dragon. I don't want any other presents. In fact, if I can have a dragon, I don't even mind not getting any presents next Christmas, either.'

Level 1 questions to ask your child

Which part of the story did you like best?
Who did you like best in the story and why?
Who didn't you like and why?
Did you think any of the words were interesting or unusual?
What do you think will happen next?

Level 2 questions to ask your child

Characters

Would you like Jilly as a friend? Why?
What sort of person do you think Mr Tonks is?
How do you think Ben feels about his sister wanting a dragon?

Important parts of the story

Why does Jilly want a dragon?
Would you like to have a dragon? Why/Why not?
What is the secret that Ben nearly gives away?

Questions inviting speculation

Who do you think Jilly wants the dragon to puff smoke at?
Do you think Jilly gets her dragon?
What do you think will happen if she does?

Reading test assessment

Level 1

Reading with accuracy, fluency and understanding
In his/her reading of the story, your child recognised familiar words, and used knowledge of letters and sound–symbol relationships in order to read words and to establish meaning when reading aloud. In these activities, he/she sometimes required support.

Understanding and response
Supported by your questions, your child responded to the story by identifying aspects he/she liked or found interesting.

Level 2 Grade C

Reading with accuracy, fluency and understanding
Your child read more than 90 per cent of the passage independently and most of this reading was accurate. His/her use of strategies was sometimes inappropriate for the task, for example starting to sound out a familiar sight word. Your child read from word to word and paused to talk about the text or to confirm meaning.

Understanding and response
Your child commented on obvious characteristics, for example was able to recognise stereotyped good/bad characters. Any retelling of the story may have been rather short or too long and heavily reliant on looking at the passage.

Level 2 Grade B

Reading with accuracy, fluency and understanding
Your child's reading was almost entirely accurate and well paced in parts of the passage, taking some account of punctuation. He/she was able to read ahead. Your child sometimes noticed when the reading did not make sense, for example by self-correcting or making an attempt to resolve the problem, even if an unhelpful strategy was repeated.

Understanding and response
Your child commented on setting and on how the plot linked or contained surprises. Your child's retelling of the story referred to most of the main events and characters, although it relied more on having remembered the shared part of the reading than on the passage read alone.

Level 2 Grade A

Reading with accuracy, fluency and understanding
The reading of the passage was accurate and your child tackled unfamiliar words with encouragement only. Your child noticed when the reading did not make sense, and took appropriate action, for example self-corrected, looked back/forward in the text, or asked for meaning. The pace and fluency of your child's independent reading showed confidence, an ability to read ahead and the use of expression and intonation to enhance meaning.

Understanding and response
Your child was able to identify and comment on the main characters and how they related to one another. He/she was able to respond when questioned about extensions or alternatives to events and actions, and about feelings created by the story. Your child's retelling of the story was balanced and clear.

Writing test

Performance descriptions for Levels 1 to 2A

Writing which does not meet the requirements for Level 1 is nonetheless likely to show evidence of some attainment. For example, your child may use single letters or groups of letters to represent meaningful words or phrases, with some control over the size, shape and orientation of the writing, and be able to say what the writing means. The attainment of such children should be recorded as **W**.

Level 1
The writing communicates meaning through simple words and phrases. In his/her reading of the writing, or in the writing itself, your child begins to show awareness of how full stops are used. Letters are usually clearly shaped and correctly orientated.

Level 2C
The writing communicates meaning beyond a simple statement. It shows some characteristics of narrative or non-narrative writing but the form may not be sustained. Individual ideas are developed in short sections. Overall, the writing draws more on the characteristics of spoken language than on written language. There is some evidence of punctuation conventions being used to demarcate units of meaning. Some common words are spelt correctly and alternatives show a reliance on phonic strategies, with some recall of visual patterns. Handwriting is legible, despite inconsistencies in orientation, size and use of upper and lower case letters.

Level 2B
The writing communicates meaning, using a narrative or non-narrative form with some consistency. Sufficient detail is given to engage the reader, and variation is evident in both sentence structure and word choices which are sometimes ambitious. The organisation reflects the purpose of the writing, with some sentences extended and linked through connectives other than 'and'. There is evidence of some sentence punctuation. In spelling, phonetically plausible attempts reflect growing knowledge of whole word structure, together with an awareness of visual patterns and recall of letter strings. Handwriting is clear, with ascenders and descenders distinguished, and generally upper and lower case letters are not mixed within the word.

Level 2A
The writing communicates meaning in a way which is lively and generally holds the reader's interest. Some characteristic features of the chosen form of narrative or non-narrative writing are beginning to be developed. Links between ideas or events are mainly clear and the use of some descriptive phrases adds detail or emphasis. Growing understanding of the use of punctuation is shown in the use of capital letters and full stops to mark correctly structured sentences. Spelling of many common monosyllabic words is accurate, with phonetically plausible attempts at longer, polysyllabic words. Handwriting shows accurate and consistent letter formation.

MATHEMATICS

Testing your child's mathematics

These notes are to help you to use this part of the book to the best advantage. They explain the ideas behind the maths test, the contents of the test material and the ways in which it may be used.

The maths section is in two parts. The first part is a Key Stage 1 type assessment, and the second part contains practice pages of questions graduated according to Attainment Targets and the National Curriculum Level descriptions.

Using the material

The test and the practice pages may be used in different ways but the most obvious will be:

1. To set the test itself first, and then base revision work from the practice section on the information found.
2. Work through the practice exercises first and then set the test.
3. A combination of the first two options; first some revision, possibly on a particular Attainment Target or Level, and then the assessment, followed by some more practice/revision.

The Practice Test

The test is not intended to be an absolute look-alike for the real thing and we have included a wide range of questions which essentially cover all of Levels 2 and 3. However, they do contain the same sorts of questions as those used at the end of Key Stage 1 and are presented on the page in a similar way so as to familiarise your child with the style of questions and so on.

The practice section also follows the general pattern of moving through the Attainment Targets level by level: it is organised on the following basis:

- Pages 52–53 Number and Algebra Level 2
- Pages 54–55 Number and Algebra Level 3
- Pages 56–57 Shape, Space and Measure Level 2
- Pages 58–59 Shape, Space and Measure Level 3
- Page 60 Handling Data Level 2
- Page 61 Handling Data Level 3

Setting the practice test

The test is fairly long for a young child and it is optional whether or not your child should sit the test in one session. You may wish to set the test in two or three stages over a period of a few days. The important thing is that your child should realise there is a certain formality about the situation which they may not be used to, although you do have some freedom to assist your child. By being flexible about the time allowance of the assessments it is hoped that your child will be able to give of their best without becoming tired. It is usually fairly obvious when children have achieved what they can.

You may wish to set the test over a three day period with the Number element being first, followed by the Shape, Space and Measure and then the Handling Data.

The test should take place in a quiet atmosphere and you may may assist your child by reading the questions to him/her although this does not include explanations of words or terms which may not be understood. This last point can be upsetting to parents who are used to assisting children, especially the younger ones, but the assessment is fairly formal and opportunities to explain something which has not been understood can come later.

For all of the work in this book, the only equipment needed is a pencil and a rubber. At no point is a calculator required.

Some problems involving working with numbers are intended to be answered mentally, and these questions do not have a working out box. Other questions require your child to show their working and these have a box for them to do the calculations — this can be explained to your child before the test begins.

Finally, the test is intended to help your child prepare for the Key Stage 1 Assessments and so should be looked on in a fairly formal way. However, it should not be a frightening experience for the child and will hopefully be looked on as an enjoyable and different experience.

Marking the practice test

A simple marking scheme goes with the test, which has a total possible score of 54 marks. A general guide is given to the marks and how they match up with the National Curriculum Levels.

Interpreting the results

Unlike the official assessments, the main point of this test is not to end up with one level description grade for your child but rather to allow them to practice assessments and show you where they have succeeded or failed and will require help. It is therefore more important to have an accurate knowledge of where your child is failing and a general feeling of how they fit against level descriptions than simply to know which level they are.

Your child does not need to have every part of the questions at any level correct in order to achieve that level or the next one. It is possible for a child to have some questions wrong at Level 2 and still achieve Level 3.

The practice pages

The practice pages are highly focused in order to give extra assessments on specific points within the Key Stage 1 mathematics curriculum. The pages themselves are based upon the National Curriculum and each page can be seen as an assessment within itself.

Test marking grid

Question Number	Possible Mark	Actual Mark	Question Number	Possible Mark	Actual Mark
1	1		16	2	
2	3		17	1	
3	1		18	1	
4	3		19	4	
5	4		20	1	
6	3		21	1	
7	1		22	1	
8	2		23	3	
9	1		24	1	
10	3		25	1	
11	3		26	1	
12	1		27	1	
13	1		28	1	
14	1		29	2	
15	2		30	3	

These marks compared with Levels are only approximate indicators.

- 0–9 Level 1 or below
- 10–19 Working within Level 1
- 20–29 Working towards Level 2
- 30–39 Working within Level 2 towards Level 3
- 40–54 Working within Level 3/Achieved Level 3

MATHEMATICS

Test

1 Circle the <u>three</u> numbers that add up to make 14

4

7

8

3

---

2 Join the sums to the correct answers

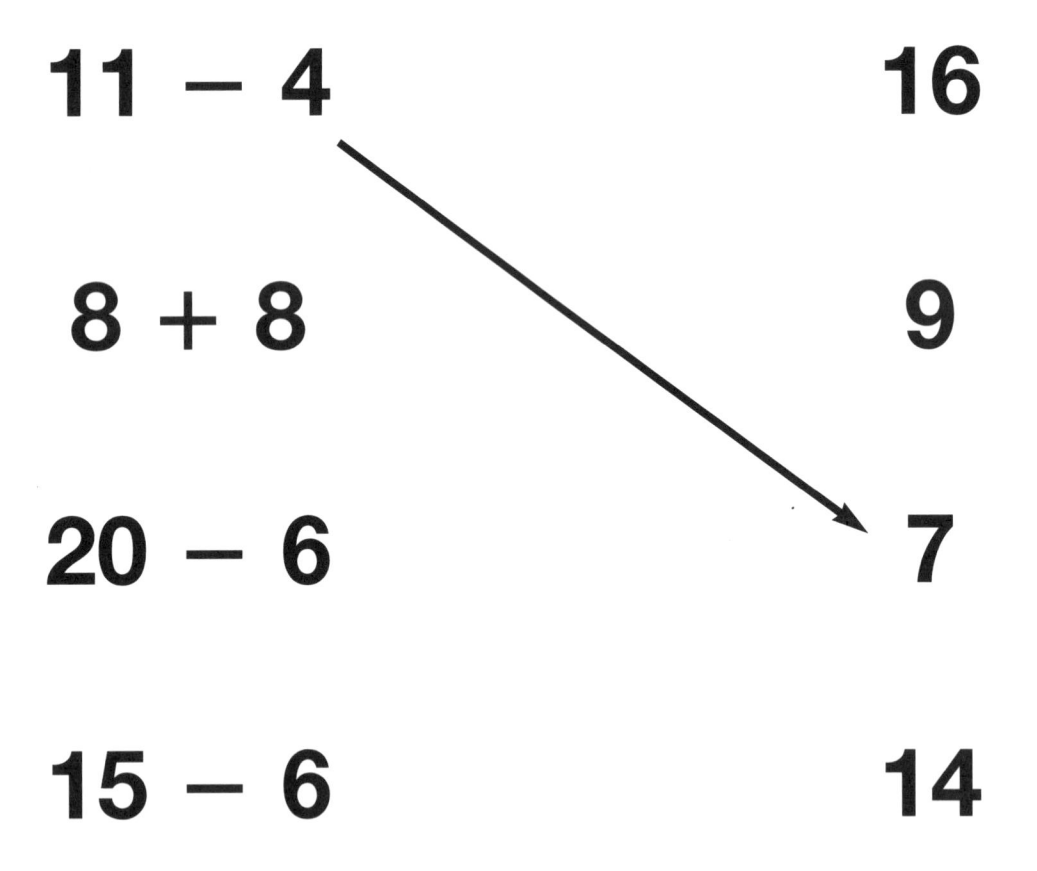

11 − 4   16

8 + 8   9

20 − 6   7

15 − 6   14

3

11p    26p    23p    16p

Tony can buy 3 things for exactly 50p.
Which 3 things ?

```
┌─────────────────────────────────┐
│                                 │
└─────────────────────────────────┘

┌─────────────────────────────────┐
│                                 │
└─────────────────────────────────┘

┌─────────────────────────────────┐
│                                 │
└─────────────────────────────────┘
```

4

6   2

A. Make the largest number you can from the two numbers.

B. Make the smallest number you can from the two numbers.

C. Subtract the smallest number from the largest number.

Answer =

Test

5 Shade in a quarter ($\frac{1}{4}$) of each shape.

A.

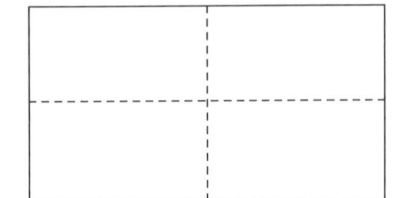

B.

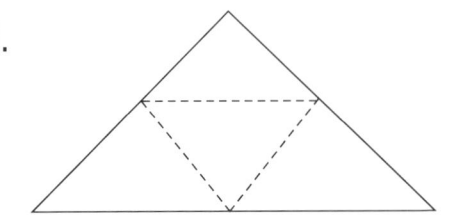

C.

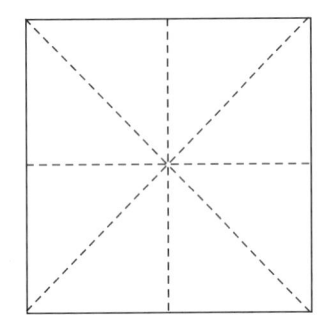

D.

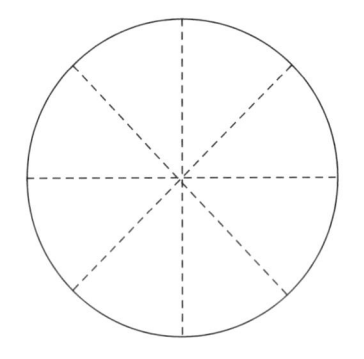

---

6 Which numbers come next?

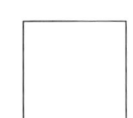

A. 3,   5,   7,   ☐ , ☐

B. 14, 12, 10, ☐ , ☐

C. 3,   6,   9,   ☐ , ☐

Test

7

Tariq wins 3 marbles from Mary.
Tariq now has 14 marbles.

How many marbles did Tariq start with?

Answer =

8 Put a different number in each box.

A. ☐ + ☐ + ☐ = **11**

B. ☐ − ☐ = **4**

Test

9 Write in the box the numbers that can be exactly divided by 2

31 10 17 14 18 62 25

---

10 Join the two numbers which make a total of 72.

24   36

44

38

26   48

Test

11 Join the sum to the correct answer

3 × 4   30

6 × 5   16

2 × 8   12

---

12 17 ÷ 3

Tick the correct answer

3 r 8 ☐   4 r 5 ☐

5 r 2 ☐   6 r 2 ☐

13 Arrange these numbers in order.

320   **23**   **230**   **32**

☐ ☐ ☐ ☐

smallest first

---

14 Finish joining the amounts

£62.00 — Six pounds twenty pence

£2.60 — Sixty two pounds

£6.20 — Two pounds sixty pence

£2.06 — Two pounds six pence

Test

15 A.

13 + 14 + 15 =

B.

70 − 24 =

16

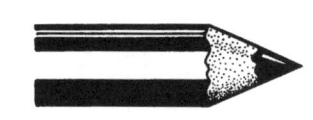

12p 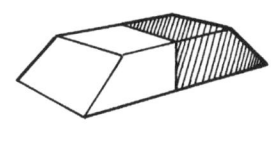   16p 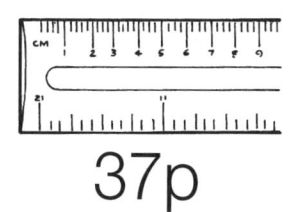   37p

Add up this list

2 pencils =

1 rubber =

1 ruler =

TOTAL

17 Where do the shapes go?

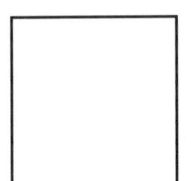

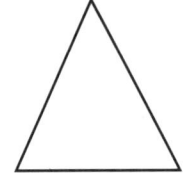

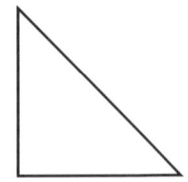

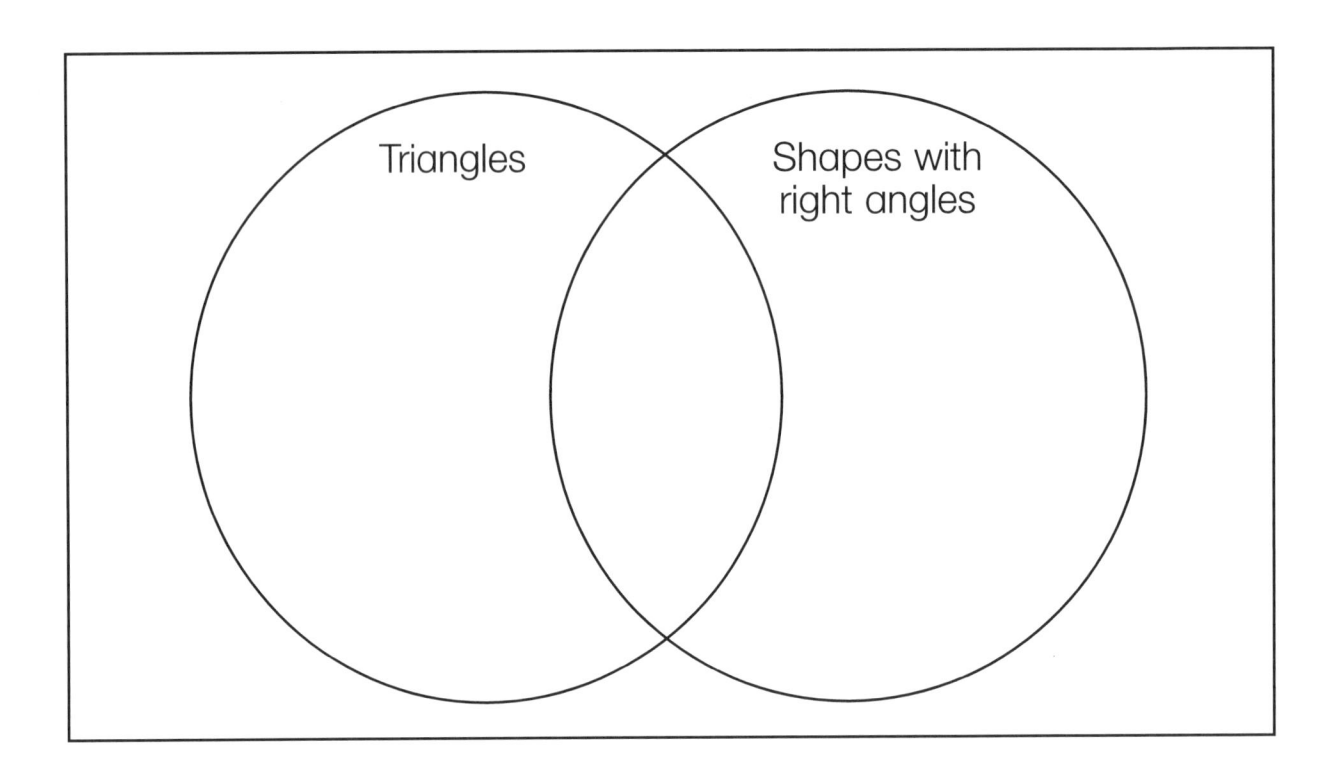

18 Put an x in the shape which has no reflective symmetry.
Use a mirror if you want to.

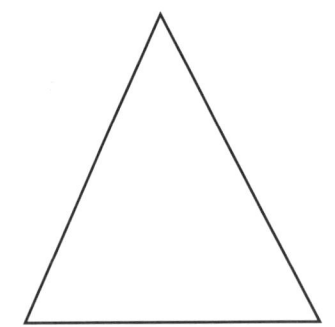

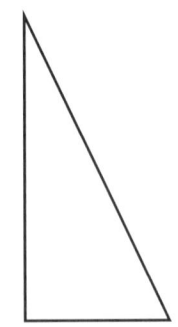

Test

19 Tick (✔) the correct answer

A. [3cm] or [3mm]

B. [1g] or [1kg]

C. [2m] or [2cm]

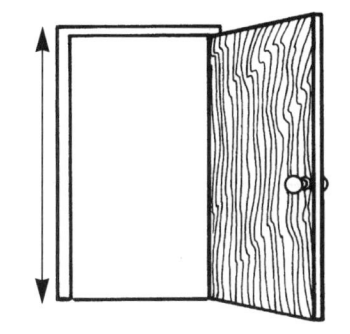

D. [170m] or [170mm] or [170cm]

---

20 Put a ring around the right angles

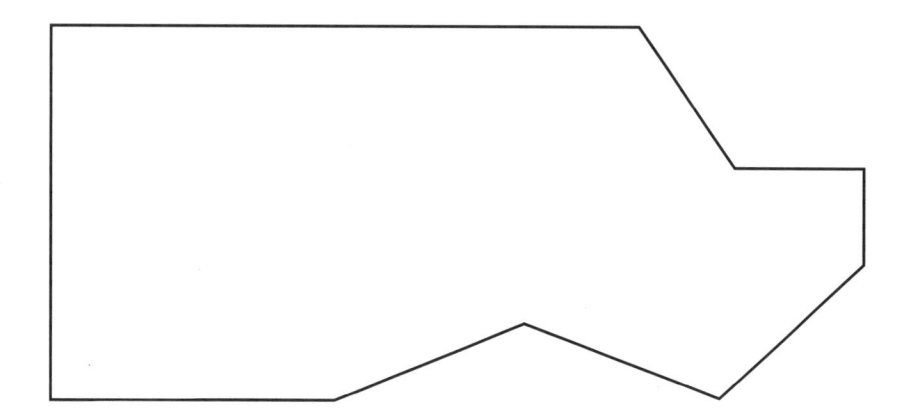

45

Test

21 Tick (✔) the shape which has just two lines of symmetry

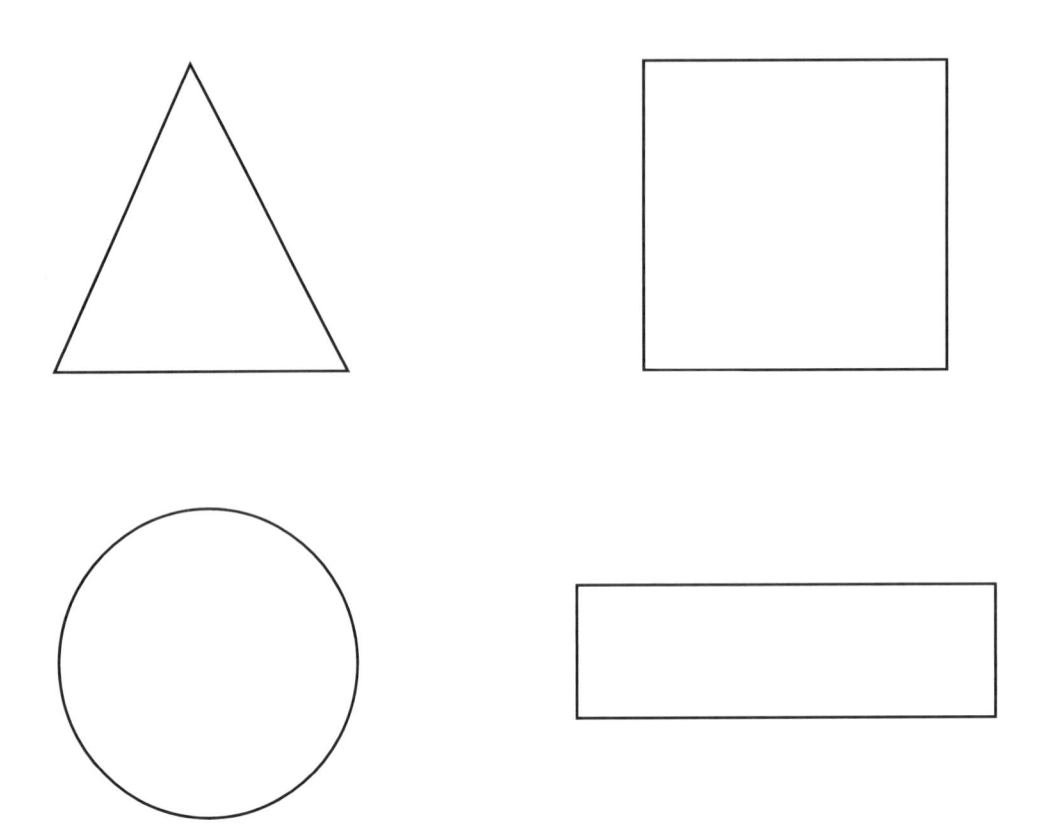

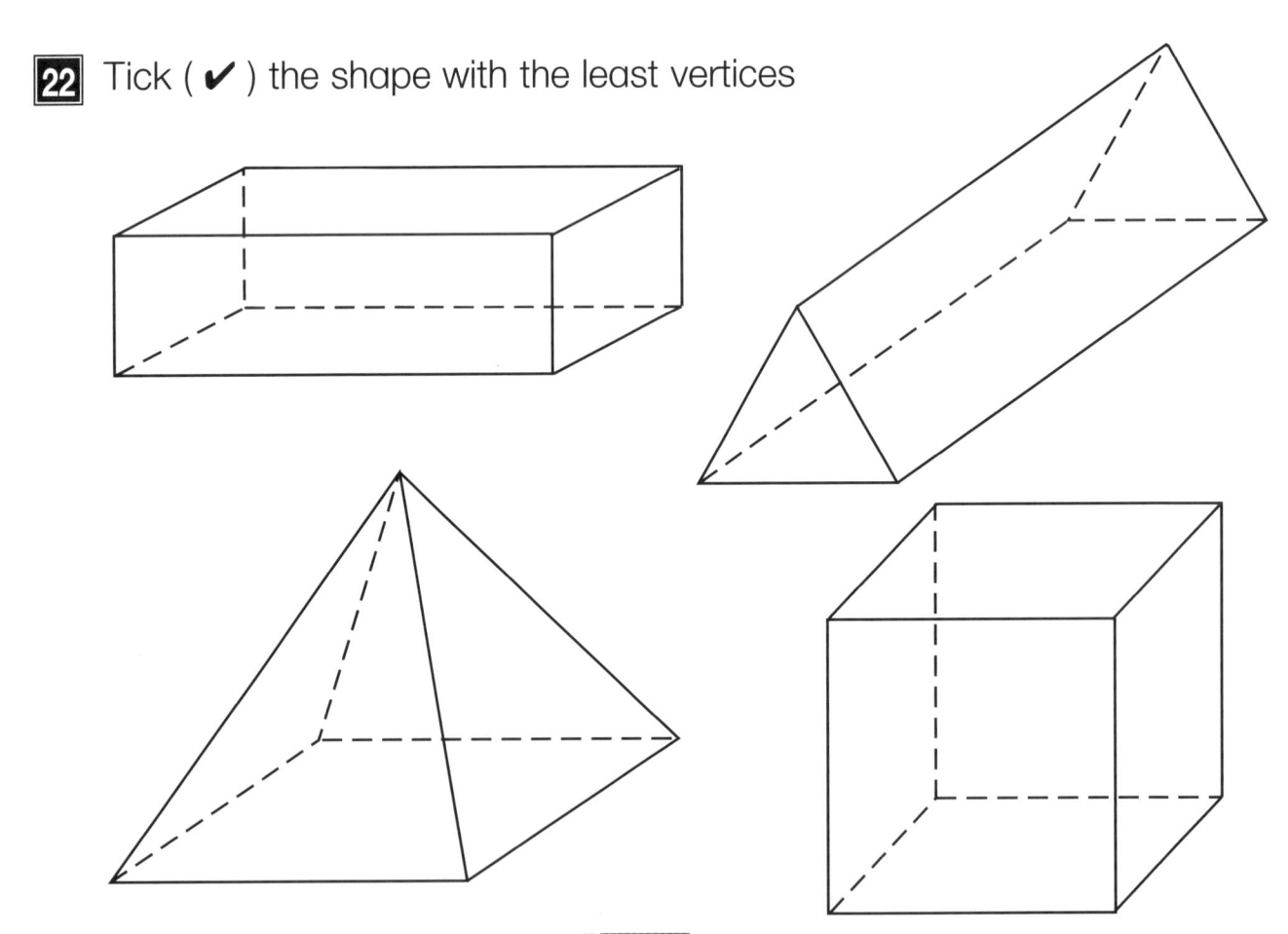

22 Tick (✔) the shape with the least vertices

46

Test 1

23 Match the clock faces by joining them

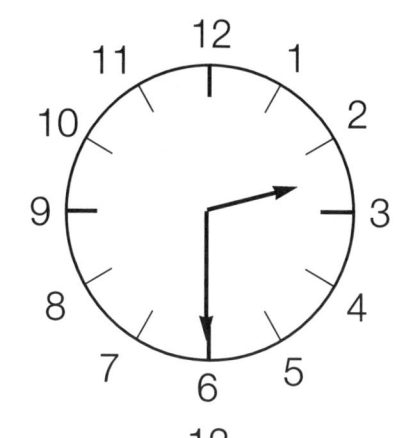

6:45

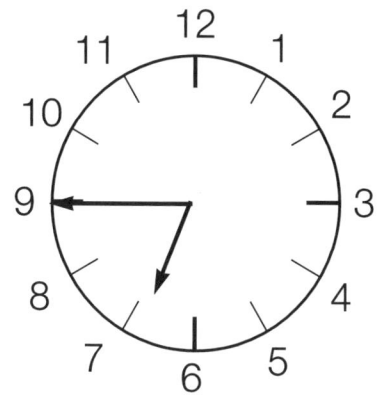

11:20

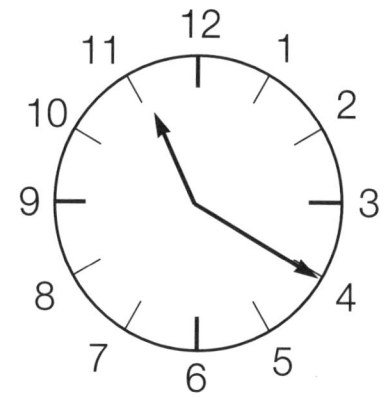

2:30

24 Tick (✔) the boxes which are true.

1 litre is the same as 1000 millilitres ☐

$\frac{1}{2}$ kilometre is the same as 250 metres ☐

$1\frac{1}{2}$ metres is the same as 150 centimetres ☐

Test

25

| Elephant | Polar bear | Tiger | Penguin |

Put the animals in the table

Animals from cold countries	Animals from hot countries

26 Which animal is in the wrong list?

Animals which fly	Animals which swim
Eagle	Shark
Sparrow	Fish
Whale	Dolphin

Test

27

30p   24p   32p

Complete this list –

ITEM	PRICE
CHOCOLATE	32p
CRISPS	

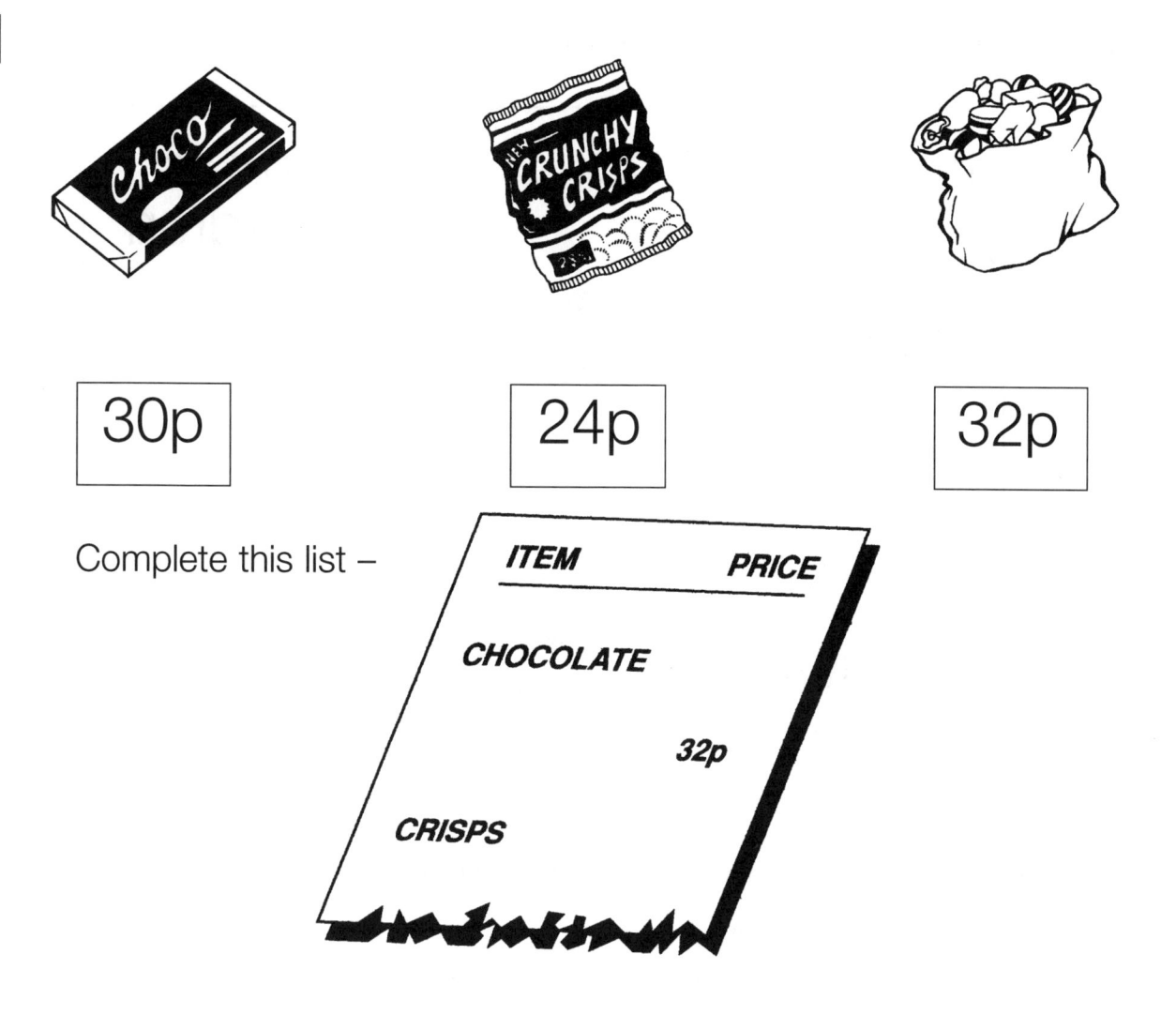

28 ☺ means 1 child

Favourite season

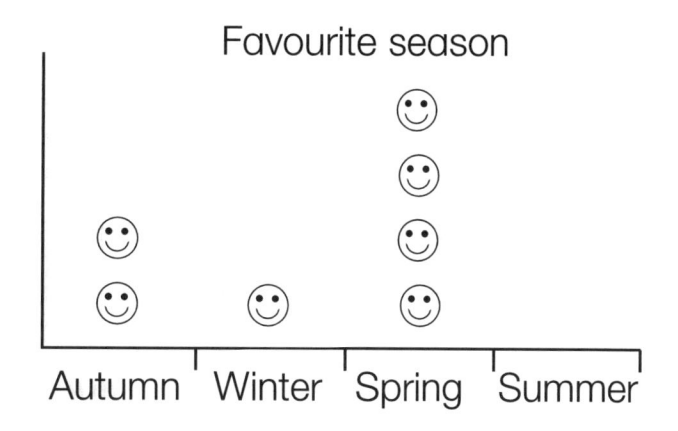

```
                    ☺
                    ☺
        ☺           ☺
        ☺    ☺      ☺
      Autumn Winter Spring Summer
```

Two children like the summer.

Show this on the pictogram.

29 This table shows the favourite fruits of a class

Favourite fruits	Number of children
Apple	5
Banana	6
Orange	4
Strawberry	12

A. More children liked strawberries than apples.

How many more?

Answer =

B. How many children are in the class?

Answer =

30 These are the scores in a house competition

House	Score
Blues	12
Reds	8
Yellows	13
Greens	7

A. Which house came second?

B. Which house had 8 points?

C. How many more points did yellows have than greens?

MATHEMATICS
Practice pages

Number and algebra Level 2

1 Write the numbers in order - smallest first

31   **24**   **50**

13

42   **85**

☐ ☐ ☐ ☐ ☐ ☐

---

2 Fill in the missing numbers

A. **6 + ☐ = 12**

B. **13 − ☐ = 9**

C. **☐ + 8 = 14**

Number and algebra Level 2

3 Put the numbers in the correct list

17   14   8   2   9   13

Odd Numbers	Even Numbers

4 Shade in half of each shape

A.

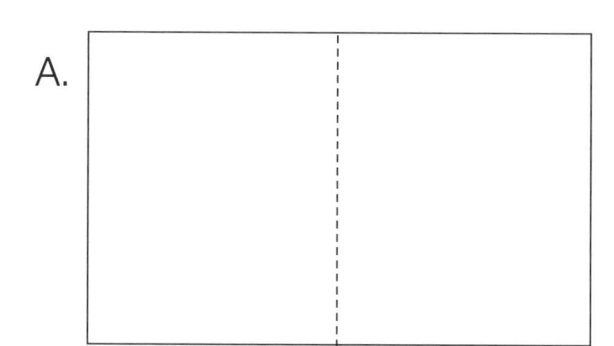

B.

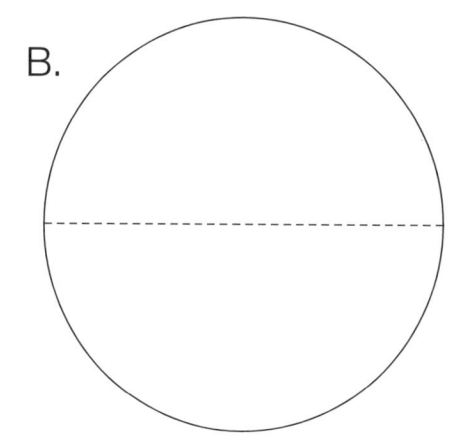

C.

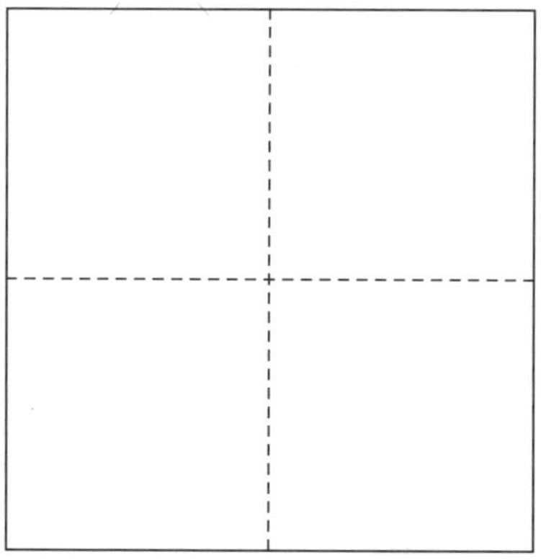

D.

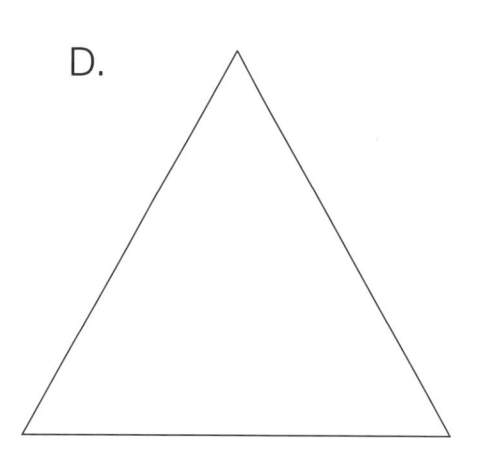

Number and algebra Level 3

1 Write the numbers that can be exactly divided by 5 in the box

20   31   52   45   75   58

---

2 Put a tick (✔) if the sum is correct.

Put a cross (✘) if the sum is wrong.

A.   36 + 44 = 80   ☐

B.   91
     −35
     ―――
     64   ☐

C.   20 + 30 + 44 = 94   ☐

Number and algebra Level 3

3 Which of these calculator displays shows 'three pounds seven pence'.

A. `000003.70`

B. `000003.07`

C. `000030.07`

---

4 Which thermometer shows 3° below zero?

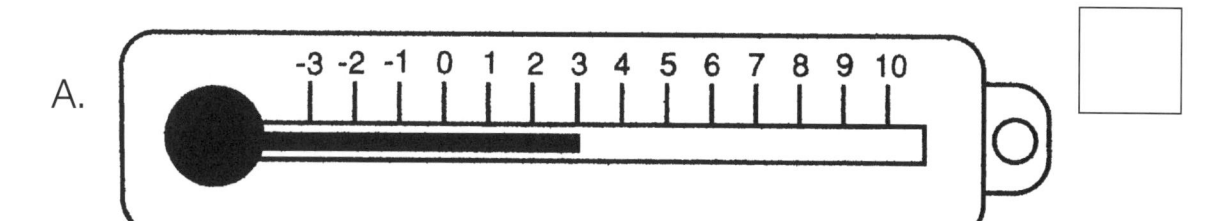

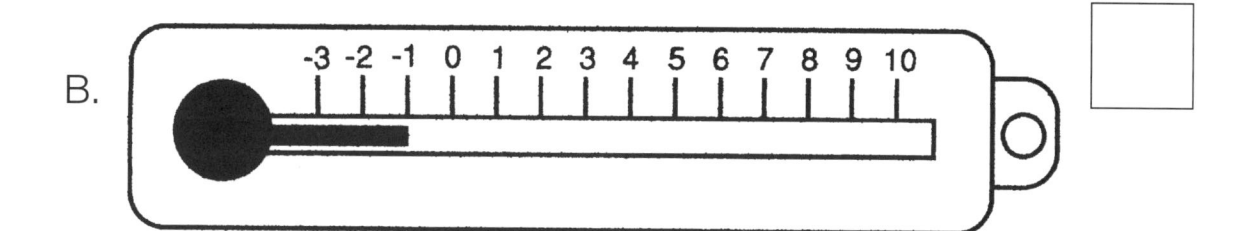

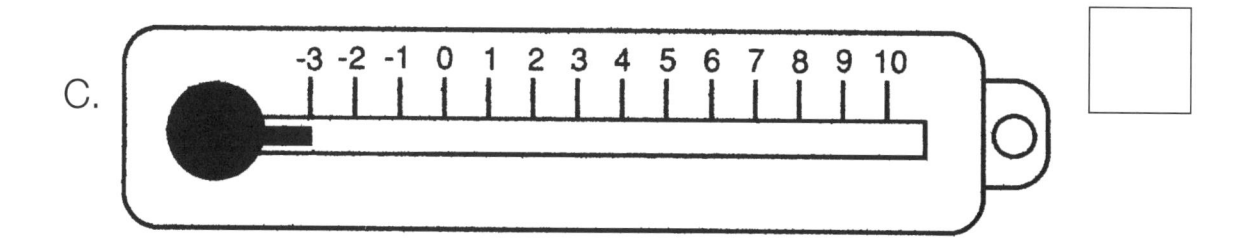

A. [thermometer showing 3]

B. [thermometer showing -1]

C. [thermometer showing -3]

Shape, space and measure Level 2

1

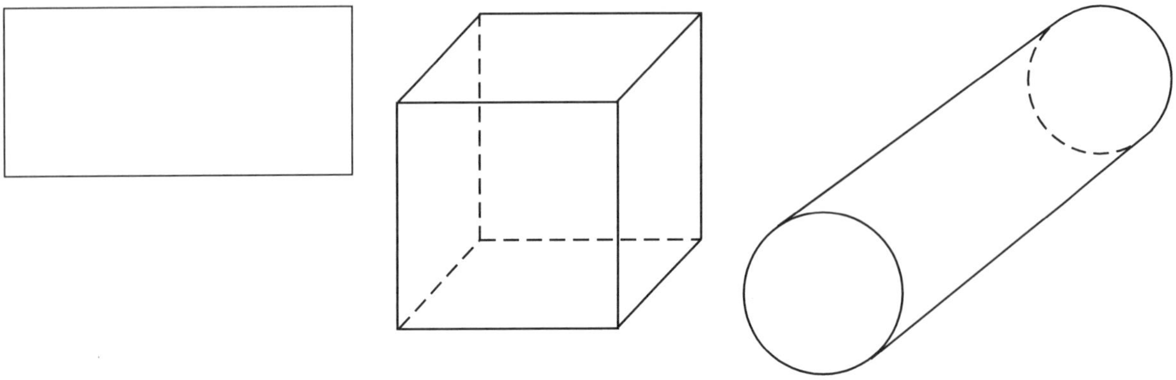

A. How many edges does the cube have?

B. Name the shape with a curved surface.

C. Which shape has 4 corners?

D. Which shape can roll?

---

2 Draw a triangle with a right angle.

Shape, space and measure Level 2

3 Estimate how long each line is

A. ▬▬▬   ▢ cm

B. ▬▬▬▬▬▬▬▬▬   ▢ cm

C. ▬   ▢ mm

D. ▬▬   ▢ mm

---

4 Tick (✔) the shapes without right angles.

A.  [rectangle] ▢

B. 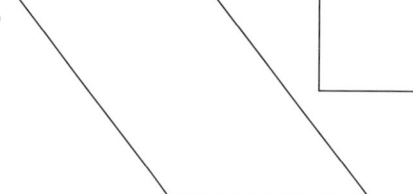 [parallelogram] ▢

C. 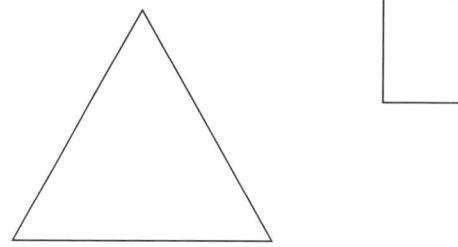 [triangle] ▢

D. 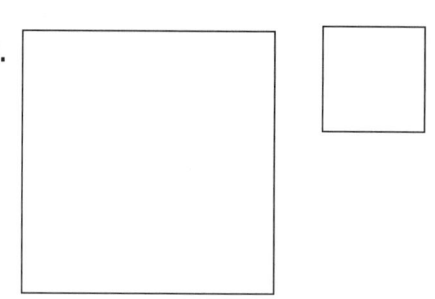 [square] ▢

E. 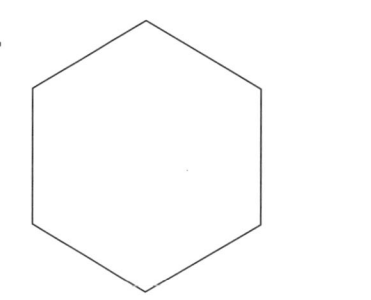 [hexagon] ▢

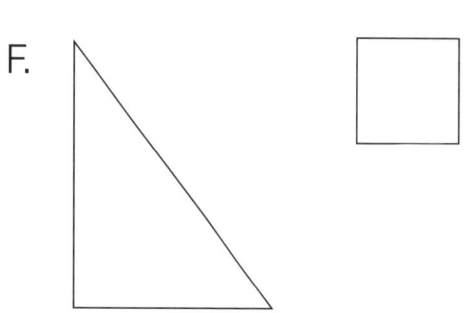

F. [right triangle] ▢

Shape, space and measure Level 3

1 Draw three lines of symmetry on this triangle

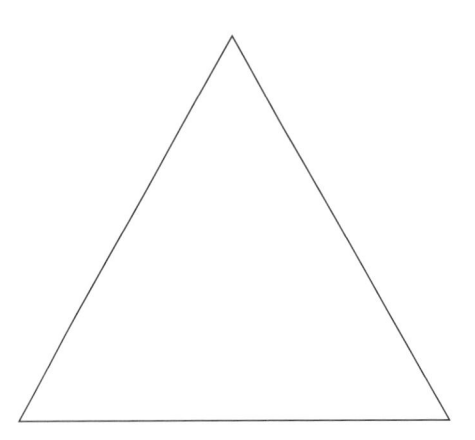

2 Which shape has the least faces? ☐

A.

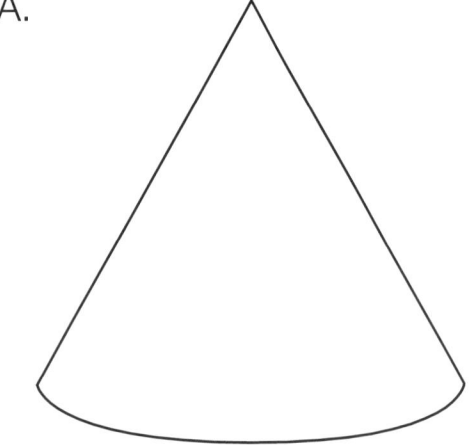

B.

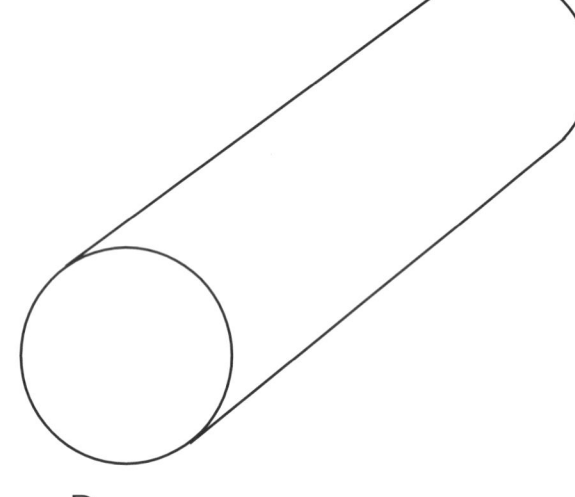

C.

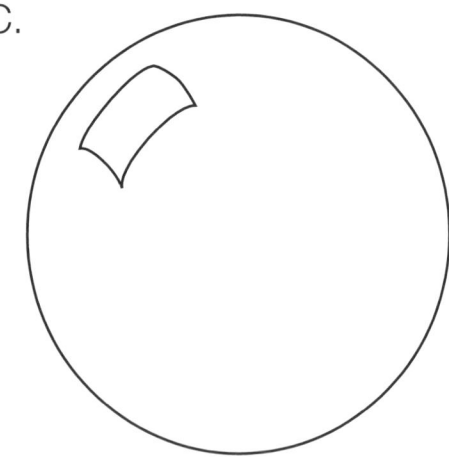

D.

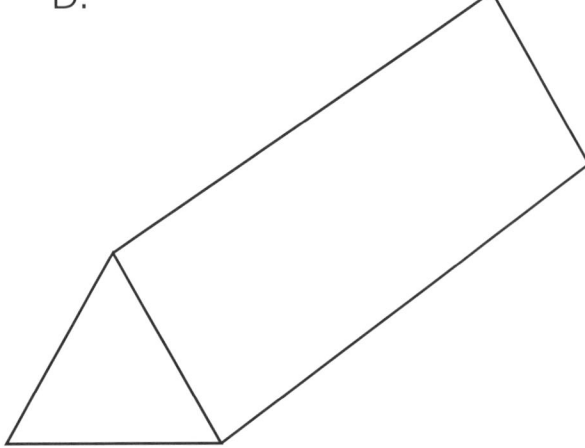

Shape, space and measure Level 3

3 Morag goes to the library at 11.15.

This is the time now

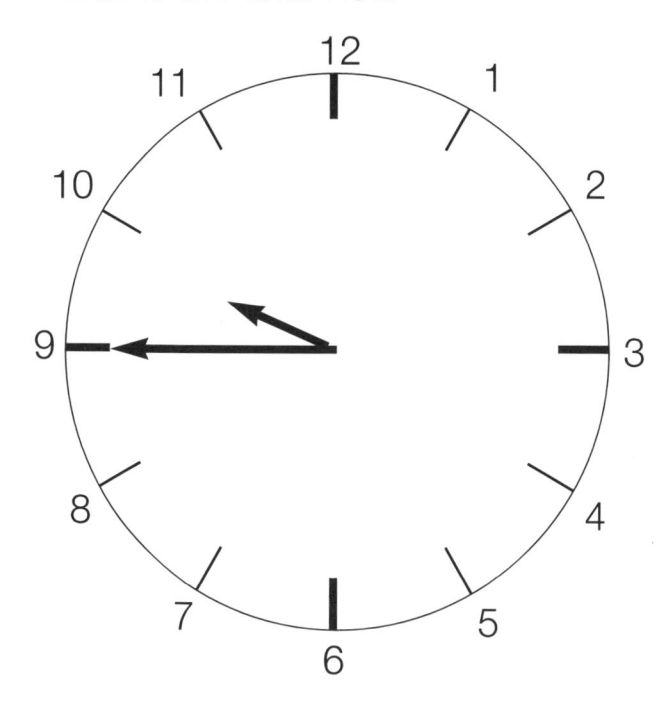

How long before Morag goes to the library? ☐

---

4 Put the units in order - smallest first.

A. Centimetre   metre   millimetre
   ☐   ☐   ☐

B. Minute   second   hour
   ☐   ☐   ☐

Handling data Level 2

1 Put a tick (✔) in the shapes which only have straight sides.

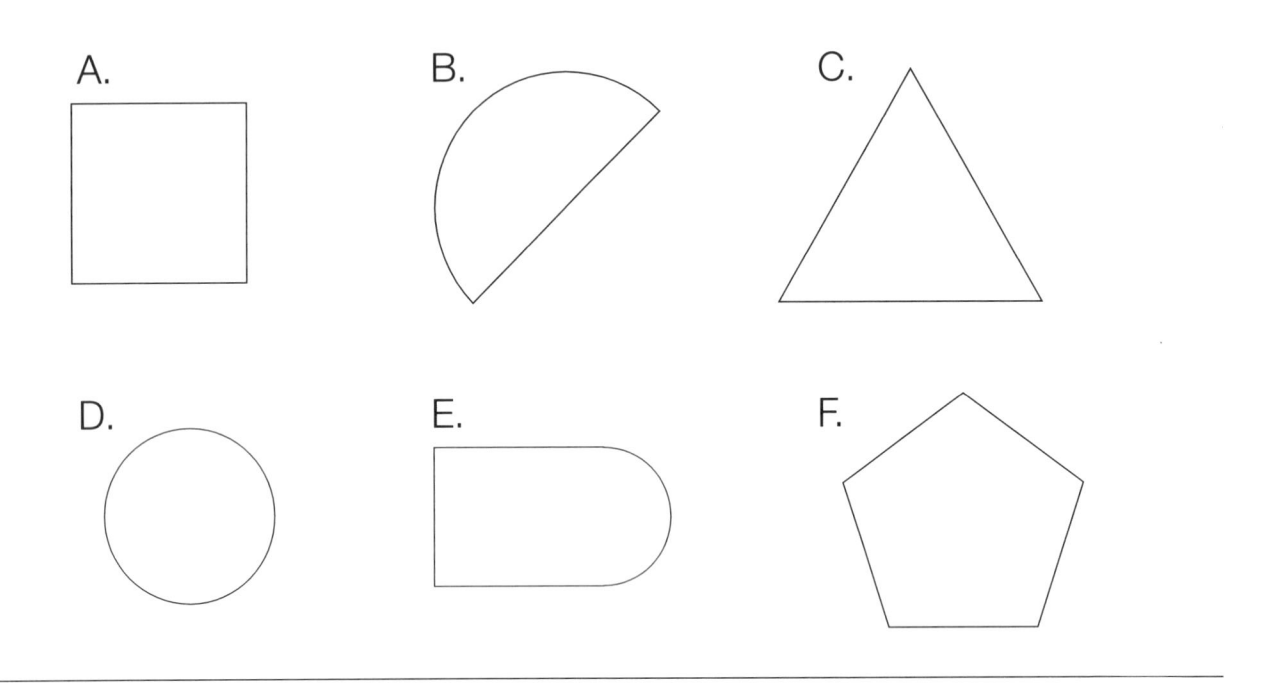

A.

B.

C.

D.

E.

F.

2 This bar chart shows how long it takes children to walk to school.

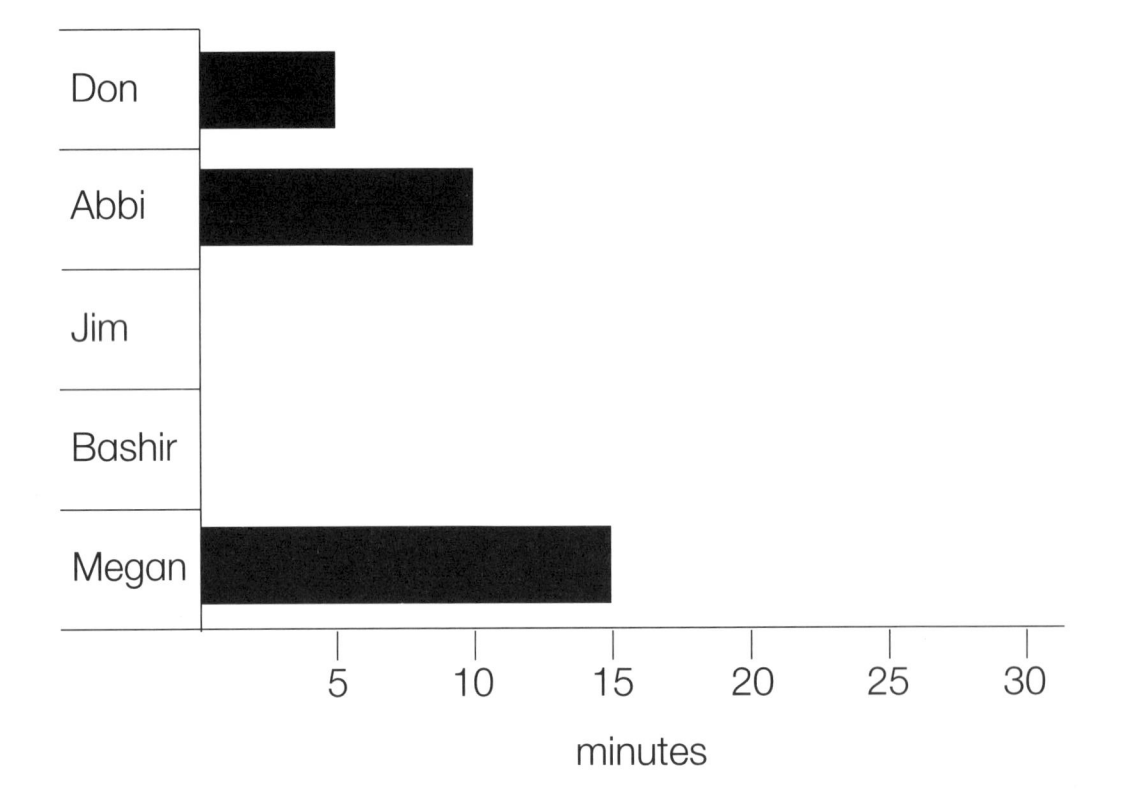

Don

Abbi

Jim

Bashir

Megan

5 10 15 20 25 30

minutes

Jim takes 25 minutes. Bashir takes 20 minutes. Show these times on the bar chart.

Handling data Level 3

1 These are the favourite types of films of some children.

Comedy – 8   Cartoons – 6   Adventure – 5

Animals – 6   Crime – 2

A. Complete this bar chart

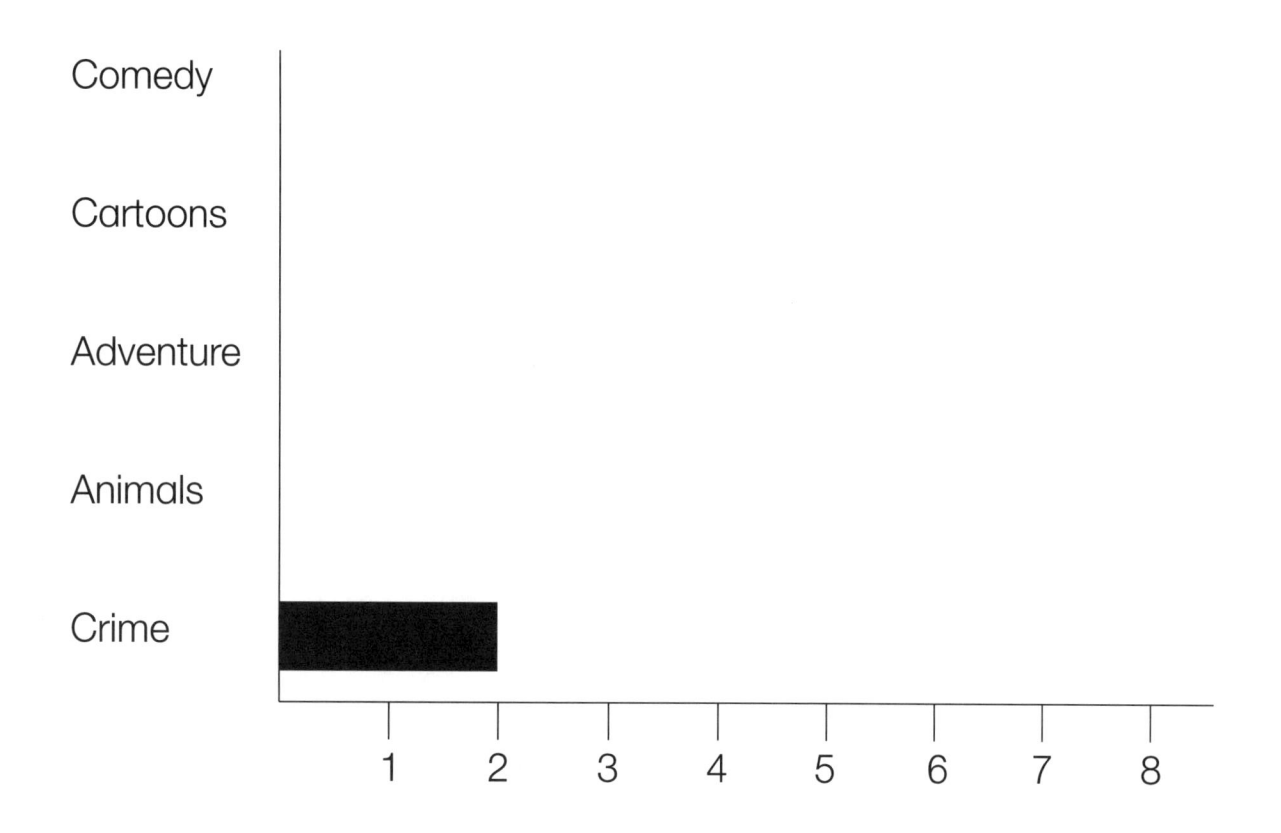

Comedy	
Cartoons	
Adventure	
Animals	
Crime	▆▆ (2)

   1 2 3 4 5 6 7 8

B. How many more children liked animal films than crime films?

MATHEMATICS ANSWERS

Test

Number - Level 2 — Pg 36
1. 4, 7 and 3 should be circled (1 mark)
2. 8 + 8 = 16, 20 - 6 = 14, 15 - 6 = 9 (3 marks)

Pg 37
3. crisps, coke, chocolate (1 mark)
4. A. 62 B. 26 C. 36 (3 marks)

Pg 38
5. Various possible answers e.g.

(4 marks)

6. A. 9 and 11 B. 8 and 6 C. 12 and 15 (3 marks)

Pg 39
7. 11 marbles (1 mark)
8. Various possible answers (2 marks)

Number - Level 3 — Pg 40
9. 10, 14, 18, 62 only (1 mark)
10. 24 and 48 (3 marks)

Pg 41
11. 3 x 4 = 12, 6 x 5 = 30, 2 x 8 = 16 (3 marks)
12. 5r2 (1 mark)

Pg 42
13. 23, 32, 230, 320 (1 mark)
14. £2.60 - Two pounds sixty pence
£6.20 - Six pounds twenty pence
£2.06 - Two pounds six pence (1 mark)

Pg 43
15. A 42 B. 46 (2 marks)
16. 77p (2 marks)

Shape, Space & Measure - Level 2 — Pg 44
17.

(1 mark)

18. the right angled triangle (1 mark)

Pg 45
19. A. 3 cm B. 1kg C. 2m D. 170cm (4 marks)
20.

(1 mark)

Shape, Space & Measure - Level 3 — Pg 46
21. The rectangle (1 mark)
22. The square based pyramid (1 mark)

Pg 47
23. top clock - 2:30, middle clock - 6:45, bottom clock - 11.20 (3 marks)
24. 1litre = 1000 ml and 1½m = 150 cm (1 mark)

Handling Data - Level 2 — Pg 48
25. Cold countries - polar bear and penguin;
Hot countries - elephant and tiger (1 mark)
26. Whale (1 mark)

Pg 49
27. Choc - 30p, sweets - 32p, crisps - 24p (1 mark)
28. Two smiley faces up from 'Summer' (1 mark)

Handling Data - Level 3 — Pg 50
29. A. 7 B. 27 (2 marks)

Pg 51
30. A. Blues B. Reds C. 6 (3 marks)

Total mark = 54

MATHEMATICS ANSWERS
Practice pages

Number - Level 2	Pg 52	**1.** 13, 24, 31, 42, 50, 85 (1 mark) **2.** A. 6 B. 4 C. 6 (3 marks)
	Pg 53	**3.** odd - 9, 13, 17; even - 2, 8, 14 (1 mark) **4.** A. various possible answers (4 marks)
Number - Level 3	Pg 54	**1.** 20, 45, 75 only (1 mark) **2.** A. tick B. cross C. tick (3 marks)
	Pg 55	**3.** B (1 mark) **4.** C (1 mark)
Shape, Space & Measure - Level 2	Pg 56	**1.** A. 12 B. cylinder C. rectangle D. cylinder (4 marks) **2.** Any right angled triangle (1 mark)
	Pg. 57	**3.** A. 2cm B. 5cm C. 8mm D. 15mm (4 marks) **4.** B, C and E (1 mark)
Shape, Space & Measure - Level 3	Pg 58	**1.** (2 marks) **2.** the sphere (1 mark)
	Pg 59	**3.** 90 minutes (one and a half hours) (1 mark) **4.** A. mm, cm, m B. sec., min, hour (1 mark)
Handling Data - Level 2	Pg 60	**1.** A, C and F (1 mark) **2.** Jim - 25 min, Bashir - 20 min (1 mark)
Handling Data - Level 3	Pg 61	**1.** A. each type to correct mark B. 4 (2 marks)